SHEARSMAN

91 & 92

SUMMER 2012

EDITED BY
TONY FRAZER

Shearsman magazine is published in the United Kingdom by
Shearsman Books Ltd
Registered office: 30-31 St James Place,
Mangotsfield, Bristol BS16 9JB
(this address not for correspondence)

Correspondence address:
50 Westons Hill Drive
Emersons Green
Bristol
BS16 7DF

www. shearsman.com

ISBN 978-1-84861-217-4
ISSN 0260-8049

Subscriptions and single copies:

Current subscriptions—covering two double-issues, each around 108 pages, cost
£13 in the UK, £16 for the rest of Europe (including the Republic of Ireland), and
£18 for the rest of the world. Longer subscriptions may be had for a proportionately
higher payment, which insulates purchasers from further price-rises during the
term of the subscription.

Back issues from n° 63 onwards (uniform with this issue)—cost £8.50/$13.50
through retail outlets. Single copies can be ordered for £8.50, post-free, direct from
the press, through the Shearsman online store, or from bookstores in the UK and
the USA. Earlier issues, from 1 to 62, may be had for £3 each direct from the press,
where they are still available, but contact us for prices for a full, or partial, run.

Submissions

Shearsman operates a submissions-window system, whereby submissions are only
considered during the months of March and September, at which point selections
are made for the October and April issues respectively. Submissions may be sent
by mail or email, but email attachments—other than PDFs—are not accepted.
We aim to respond within 2–3 months of the window's closure.

Contents

NATHAN SHEPHERDSON

ten acres of silence

you sold me
ten acres of silence
telling me
i could plant our thoughts
in rows that match
these potato-stamp lines
on our foreheads . . .

weeks later
i am not surprised
to find the fruit
are vertical replicas
of your uninjected lips
capped in lace chlorophyll
and inside each
is a saliva capsule
containing what will be
on another day
two red commas . . .

the taste
wires me instantly to the day
we took a complimentary butcher's calendar
off your mother's kitchen wall
and put white sugar mounds
on our respective birth dates
swapped chairs
closed our eyes
and trying not to laugh
with our tongues hanging
impersonating new drooling limbs
we move as slowly as possible
towards what we know
^ is there ^

William & Catherine

either side of their table
William & Catherine Blake
are shelling commas

an intricate task
each one is nested in the soft v
formed with the two index fingers
the comma rested face down
under pressure from living brackets
the topographical edges of their thumbnails
meeting at their waists
to shape an efficient tool

the husk is separated from the kernel

the husks are set aside but not wasted
will be ground down to a binding agent
for use in ink in William's prints
a secret ingredient
that teaches his blacks their profound speech

& William & Catherine
regularly glance up at each other
happy that their industry
can produce the invisible sinkers
needed to weigh down the smiles
they throw in front of each other

the kernel is separated from the husk

the kernels as they usually are
are set aside in the slip ware dish
depicting the 'Pelican in her Piety'
with letters brushed and bled under the glaze
the Congreve fragment
feed thee from my own vitals

and when the quantity says so
William & Catherine unstop a homemade ale
pour it with care into a pair of tankards
as if to manufacture scales for conversation
to discuss what's wrong with the World
and to rearrange Art & Poetry as it should be

fresh commas are an aphrodisiac

and in the most intense moments
William sees words emerge on Catherine's lips
wiping them backwards on a spare page
from right to left for tomorrow's poem
to write backwards to look forwards
to spread the double landscape over their bodies
to open it wide into another prophetic book
as it lays astride the valleyskin on Catherine's chest
with Death on the left and God on the right
with their own spines two parts of the clamp
that can permit and halt this soulscythe perception

and at the end
they come upon the half grain of sand
that is more than enough
to clog a giant mind

there is no rest for the wicked
because the wicked are unable to see
where the rests were removed from their sentence
, ,

it takes as many commas
to fill a moon
as it does to build a single thought

a white shirt is

a white shirt
wind sings its hymn
to torso empty absence
absence still
dreams the collar into white lips
unspoken
dissolved through emptier tongue
it dissolves into absence
as unflesh reabsent

as absence is a planet is
we never see
until we are
where it is
a planet is
with or without sleeves
white as one held breath
it will finally not knock
at the door it will not open
until it is not the space
it does not occupy
can not be worn as the shirt
it is

it was
as cloth rumoured should be
forgotten not to be begging
at altitude from our eyes made
bleached azalea white
our eyes could this shirt fold
against its will
tourniqueted around light its own
restrict to the bodyknot
birth with no memory no
form into fact and vanishing
is into into is
is into is

is a shirt
not an actor to become
at any stage
of its existence
is not an actor
if it exists
it exists if
if it exists
is not a shirt

is this and
is this and
this and is the woman is
who air removed from shirt
who breathed did no life
air who is air is soaked
into the lisp in transparent
soaked from shirt beneath
blood two spots
were his nipples were once
two bloods grow
once she eyes closes
once burning the shirt is

the itch

for Hamish Sewell

having stuffed the chicken
with the pages of a Russian novel
i realize i've used the wrong chapter

perhaps i should admit
i never read it
in the first place
second time around

i won't read it either
because the wine is open
the oven's at the correct temperature
and the guests are at the door

as the proverb says . . .
"the itch
won't fail the thought
calling for help
under the skin"

surface

i murdered a line
in Bridget Riley's eye

without alteration
to the optical blackmail
in satisfied heads
the colour
has weighed the hand
that put it there

a surface
divided by the object
is the surface
divided by the object

SAM SAMPSON

All the Everlasting Cataracts

After John Keats' Hyperion

near at hand

rip-cords surround the centre

gurge of pulse

on / oft

to sometimes detect
actual remnants

to look up, and tell of this fractal shape

one gradual solitary star
which comes upon silence

...

fragments_____

that word startled up

filled in, in pencil
a transcript: the story dawned   outlines

nerveless, script-less, dead-

ends felt in every feature
eyes closed: bowed head listening to the earth

to an ever-revolving spiel

...

trace : tracer
           one of two great circles
                  intersection: right angles at poles
      nadir: the low
zenith   the high
     circles and arcs
         broad-belting colure

sages, keen-eyed astrologers
earth-bound evangelists

    they study the sky
        study the fault lines

(the god and sunrise)

    both, and both in one
all along a dismal rack of clouds

upon the boundaries of day and night
  a drifting mass

    cloud
    on
    cloud

      the sky in-
        verse

         …

        nineteenth century

    slow-breathed melodies,
like a rose in vermeil tint and shape

enter, but who entertains?
        effigies, visions, extras…

opaline forms
amorphous

:   pictures of intimacy

all the everlasting cataracts

... pools

loops   these crystalline pavilions
pure fields mantled by sea salt

...

re-cast the self-
same beat

in hollow shells

in the cadence of time
where a dead branch fell, there did it rest...

reset to follow, to turn and lead the way

a stream went voiceless by   (streamed)

mountainous: no shape extinguishable

when the bleak-gown pines
when winter lifts his voice, a noise

the mysterious grate of wind in trees
whether in calm or storm

(the same scene)

god of the sky : bookish séance

that old spirit-leaved book
sifted well … from the ion-universe

…

flames yield like mist

all calm through chaos and darkness
from chaos and darkness

the extraordinary

the constant…the inter-
nal law   and how
I

whether through conviction, or disdain
in this expressive line
quicken the patter of beads

(pearl beads drop-
ping from their string

ele-
mental nature
powerful similes

ponderous millstones)

...

appearance of strength
a deception masking real weakness

essence in its tent

before the winged thing

silver wings of dawn rising
now a silver line hints at this approach

in each face a glint of light
see how the light breaks in with this line

(haphazardly)

till suddenly a splendour
like morning

the horizon in noise

...

at the set of sun
light fades
first from the eastern sky

to one who travels from the dusking east
attributes of the wanderer

wondering in vain about
the inventor of god and music

of light and song

soft breaking noise
>> white melodious throat

>> a name signifies memory
> would come as no mystery

>> pin-pricks of the world ... name-sakes

>> for me variance
> by knowledge only

the above and the below

>> gathering all things mortal
> this endless commencing

>> this still,
>> steady light

> brilliance
of the moon   O

>> independence
> acknowledges no allegiance.

KAREN LEPRI

Curvature

Your hand cups
    space, the shortest

distance no longer
    an option: black hole's

               Eros

Animal, fallible
    we scenic slip
round each

               Necks of

Light
    bowed when
the gasping

               Stops

Is it getting bigger
    or smaller,
she

               Asks

Warping toward another

Dust

        & your body

nests in the house's

        corners. Shuttle-cocked

            when the door opens;

                dreamdregs bound

            in unbinding

        form. Rest

a handful over one

        then a mouthing. I

            lash down, saddle

                back, shuck the rough

            unholding you.

Ether

slipping amid machinery
        dragged by lead

arrangements of horse
        tails & light whisps

        because it was no longer possible to speak

we moved in you, and you apparent
        in us—blindness ate & waits

by the planetary pool

        way of ordering by time alone

watching small hairs fade

our restless heels
        run aground in shallows

        of simultaneous states

agreed if we could see

Dark Matter

you think

not to ask
not knowing

amid such
territory

how the dark
could be my throat

& diagram
the same

un-imagible
merengue

light mister of
void unstrung

the filial gas
of radio (my eyes

holes) waves

you mummify

keep me un-
wrappable

night the cloth
I snag closer

The Great Attractor

Within &
on top

of, each
other

risk of
blueshift

elongation
will disappear

over emphasize
you

an elective
cup to drink from

redshift
stirring

God

pointing
a little finger

from some-
where

to the spot

etched before
the gate

where you leant
pulling Williams

Light

Even you and I are waves—the distance
between our crests small as in
unimaginable, touching—

and particles—our game endless,
crashing into, feeling
substantial : contrary to law

MELISSA BUCKHEIT

Narrative

Across the wide sea
I came
and you did not recognize me
for what I appeared to be:
the rust and gray water
with its broken remnants of seaweed
rocking, slapping against the side of many pilings anchored
in the vast and realist Atlantic,
which never lied to a soul
who drowned in its waves
or pretended to be anything
other than it was—
barren at times, welcoming, others
—a challenge to the people
who settled there.
Dismal, everyone thinks we are,
like Emily Dickinson was
apparently a depressed character—solitary, too;
the weather will do that to anyone.
Inside the vast sea,
I existed for centuries,
until I came to be born
and landed on a narrow
expanse of island—as after a long trip.
We were waiting to come to America,
my parents and I,
and so the sea was our home
lodging broken remnants of ancestors' suffering
in its cold depth, like
jagged rock loose from the shore
held on our backs, then swallowed by liquid sand with the tides.
We slept there a while,
hoping we had left luggage or broken furniture behind,
useless to carry further ashore.

We came up through the Atlantic
but we were changed
and could no longer speak,
we had to learn language again.
Our sounds were rough and harsh to unfamiliar ears,
but with each other, intimately
we were shyly gentle,
our voices soft like honey.

Neva

I'm not human for you, smallest side of a pin

whom I love. Summer in Boston. Water

of the lake, blue and cold at the bottom. Akhmatova

said the cold fire of the heart. I will quote her.

"Remember me".

I am alive like the coathanger twisted for abortion.

That is not the truth, Akhmatova would say something

subtler, something about the mildness of the Neva

in winter, how her love is a shadow at dusk

moving across the sky, as it dies. My love

is not like that. I am like that

as I disappear.

Hildegard

In what lairs
we cached our nimble fingers—
secret salve of a sister's voice,
liquid, repetitive, chill like night.
No ice but stones encasing us,
rhythmic weight of candalmas,
aria, matins.

I kept my thirds hidden on rich paper,
needlepoint, whale-inked.
What passion engraved
should arise and I flush, what
floating heart, murmur
of a lover, Him / my sisters,'
a vacuum to which I faint?

We all faint. No remarkable mind
tethered above but our own breast
now bound low. Below

~

ecstasy of a third   was an herbalist, medicinal

(lived) in a box

was an animal's intestine, on fire

Antithetical Monologue

This isn't a stage upon which my dead and passed relatives play the parts of assholes and drunks, child molesters and wife-beaters, dragging themselves through me like ghosts pass through people, steam from a New York City sewer grate, the grass which refuses to grow above some graves, their energy plagued and plaguing me in intermittent moments where my body and mind try to grasp our cleaved relationship. This is the poem that begins and begins again, where I drive them from me like the demons I don't believe in, weird marble frescoed half-animal half-beasts, stabbed with the arrows of avenging angels, in Rome. Those half-humans always have their eyes rolled back in a sort of pain or terror or death. Medieval saints do too, a collective response to the presence of God. There is no religious anguish, another sacrament, as devotion to Mary and the promise of purity of soul should have fed the starving of Eire, the babes nourished on a new milk. The milk was air, the milk passed through their hands like an invisible smoke; the purses and pockets of the rich, of Catholic priests and government ministers weighed down the air, so the air was empty. A belly of air. My great-grandparents and grandparents exhausted in their own perfect suffering, their mortification of flesh, their terror and pain and death. Their heavy hands on their children's backs, their heavy tears of salt, their echoes and shadows tracking around the corners of city buildings and the glowing arcs of streetlamps at night. Their gibberish, their endless lament, their curses and they cursed. I'm alone. They almost seem dead to me.

MARTYN CRUCEFIX

After reading Hass on Miłosz

. . . if he meant "Oh!" or "O!"

But I'd be first to agree
Oh! is longer drawn already beginning
the button-down of understanding
that well-I-never

with its freighting of verb tense
and identity—
whereas O! is sudden more urgent
a rapture surely a moment rapt

when we are prised open by desire
as I am here in 'Nicolas'
where I've chosen this bottle of red
I'm not buying for myself

but for my daughter's cello teacher
now she's to be replaced
by another more challenging
or at least they say he comes trailing

an Eastern European name
like Vaclav or Pavel or is it simply Pal—
and as I stand here
handing the dark bottle across

to the assistant in her maroon vest
I hear the loose-limbed clatter of jazz
on the speakers though
it has been there all along

Ornithology or *A Night in Tunisia*
and she stares at me

with no more than the desire to serve
and sees my eyes widen

sees the tiny up-tilting of my chin
and you'd forgive her
for thinking she was the focus
of my arousing when really

she is a fragment
equal to the others no more
though no less than the fragment
I find myself smilingly O!

Apology

Tired is a frail portmanteau word
for being wound to such a pitch
as this all day tail-spin
of disrupted routines
this driving to make connections
this anxious waiting in case ourselves
and our reference details
might fail to correspond—
that our seats will or will not be vacant
our monies valued rightly
our neatly labelled luggage
man-handled on and off
the right plane no rip off no
rip off—that the hire car's OK
and of course it's not
and the boy's already burning
his ten-year-old fuse
to be slumped now and weeping
in the back seat in the dark
of what was planned to have been
our lovely sun-down coastal finish

and it's his father's tongue lashes out
to skew these closing hours
and maybe these months these years
of shame but say nothing
no more say it's nothing to him

On trust
for Milena

In lilac-blue of ageratum
the heads of tawny-black bees
delve in the dusty mouths
they see it in German

as she says *the now's today*
it is a phrase they use
the slow sikh with *tremens*
brought to table with his tray

toward an empty garden chair
the word *pigeon* flaps down
they see it in German
crumbs scattered everywhere

the pink top on her phone
the couple at their crossword
the perm eating cake
a young woman taking notes

she plumbs the English line
how it sounds in German
hearkening through a sheet
clear blue water between

the feel of fabric on her tongue
murmuring beneath a sheet
beneath a sheet the wink of eye
they see it in German

In hospital

after Boris Pasternak

As if window-shopping
crowds block the way
the stretcher swung aboard
and paramedics in place

and street shadows carved
by the ambulance's beam
a city thunders past
police and pavements dancing

and doors as much as faces
gape as the nurse's grip
on the saline bottle
loosens where she tips

to and fro as the storm
floods the gutters runs free—
paperwork in triplicate
the roar of A and E

neglected in a corridor
he snuffs at iodine smells
in the air-conditioning
all the time the ward fills

flashes of white uniform
a window holds his eye
its glimpses of a garden
beneath the rag of sky

till beginning to realise
the import of each question
these nodding heads
odds stacked against him—

supine in the glare
his gaze against a wall
the flaring of streetlamps
now weirdly grateful

he catches at blinds falling
at branches of a tree
leaves lost to the wind
are bowing him goodbye

Things are as they are
his prayer to the wall
streets death lights night
the enveloping hospital

twisting a handkerchief
my tears soaking through
these drowsy sedatives
they blur my sight of you

yet sweet to feel a light
laid on the bed to see
myself my life my living it
as gifts lent to me

to feel a hand nearby
in good time to replace
this brooch this handiwork
in death's jewel-case

LINDA RUSSO

from Flitting

Short Crisp Chip

flight call is a sharp, distinctive plick
        what is happiness?
driven out into the rain, not an ordinary rain
but the rain of unselfconsciousness
studded with letters of introduction

I am thus connected, the human right or rite
        of many centuries, a spectacle
which seems to be in conflict

the call is a short crisp chip rich with possibility

I react to people one way
        but I could react that way

Chipping

you're twirling in song or chipping, or cawing are we
speaking the same language your flat note of
inattention what brings us to this place? your see saw
your caw, your hum, scribble, your chip, your wall
of branches, you goddam three dogs barking at it all

*

what writing is indigenous to a place?
The birds punctuating the grass, perhaps
the squirrel punctuating the branch

*

the problem:

> all is awake in its own drama
> announcing my folly in this
> thing for my yard
> though it's good to see
> you green things I tended last spring
> sprouting

the lesson:

> wait

First Little Peeps

shall I go or no, how
    shall I live my life, this
collection and dispersion
    energy, the first little bird peeps arrive
with a dousing stick

by *my* I mean all that accompanies

Bird Saw

like mobile weeds sometimes
    birds chatter in the yard
growing awareness almost time for lunch
      bird song, bird saw
sunwarmed distant visual vibrato of leaves
    bird saw, bird song
left weedy

Aswarm

don't forget the sky , or what's at hand

     pears, apples, plums and nuts
     feed birds, rabbits, worms, beetles etc., squirrels
     in the next yard, too

sky brightens, dogs bark
               the sunlight is doing what?
    it's lighting   they are sunning
    it's a luminous hot spot I know little of
     a yard aswarm with aphids
    no poem follows from these lines

much of the yard is shaded at this hour

Orphan/age

On this hill, the grey almost palpable with.
Moist, the day, on my brow. Head down into.
Grief accumulating to what. She fell on the ice,
broke a wrist. An influential event. Hold out for
an attached garage. Down into my little city.
Large enough for anonymity. If I play it.
I think myself nondescript. I almost want to.
Break on ice. Most nights I wear her.
I chose three nightgowns, a couple necklaces, four.
They're cotton, gentler. The *tabula rasa* of a grey.
Not for me. If visible, if palpable, the severity of.
Wandering amid the shops, cupping aimless.
In the pub, students compare. I can't hide.
Where she never was. Cobblestones, laughter.

Divining for Starters (81)

from acute pain as though

diversion or placebo

pouring forth in a stream

the nerve endings fire and fire

a glass of red, amass the vines

mollify those little

prescription, circumscription, circumduct

embodied I—

Divining for Starters (82)

from the tourists' street

last night I broke

a *Big Issue* seller every thirty

moving through sunlight

the pale tan stone of Georgian

as though veiled

a memory of affection

in shade casting no shadow

a surge of wedding hats

dissolving yet intact—

city state

§ 1

there's beauty in this dereliction   way-
ward broken vision   merely a matter
of purity   membranes sounding out strings
vibrating by plot conjectured to a
fault   the usual nonsequiturs aligned
amid resisting concentric   raised like
a hieroglyph against a bruised pane she
said for a bailout handed to them on
whereas by these precepts only one of
many possible wavering sumptuous
adept   involved   of course how could she not
have seen it coming   not obviously
anything of the kind   a little pet-
ulant perhaps   impartially   withheld

§ 2

anticipating such scenes played out in
labyrinthine construction a stream of
moted profligate light to abandoned
seats   impervious to glass shards old brick
& dog shit in among the willow herb
where too many converge they used water
cannon loaded with liquid deodor-
ant to hose away the stench in the streets
a squeeze under way & the camera
team is there   her body occupies a
space it does not own   extrapolating
an intricate facsimile   all bets
are off whatever can be accomplished
in the projection room   no guarantees

§ 3

vapour trails in sunday evening sky war-
ranting rhetoric of happy hour warm
blooded in partial recognition of
conditions of recovery wiring
mainframe enjambment expressed these days in
bored vicarious alembic in un
tidy rooms a cheap analogy an
assailable victory just a mouse
click away for gaming pleasure now &
with the latest shader technology
to detox casserite environment
street level understated against a
wall the ultimate ego discontent
high score total enemies another beer

§ 4

accidental clocks pitching us into
fiction   the story changing over time
the official version constantly up-
dated   having regard to   rictus grins
in public spaces   the tendency of
a system to entropy   credit watch
negative   terminally risk-averse
to limit the consequences   or just
to see what happens when   the knowable
is all we have   keeping all our aspir-
ations on one side of the equation
adrift among the phonemes of a baff-
ling language & floundering   there's nothing
arbitrary in the placing of walls

§ 5

fabulation and confabulation
fallible utopias come & go
in this city where nothing rises a-
bove five or six storeys & except the odd
cupola hotel tv tower church
spires cavorting light with conspicuous
corporate purpose   coming out of that
cave with the images seared into her
retina she thought she had reali-
ty mapped that she could look medusa in
the face & not turn to stone   what she re-
membered   digital abundance   degrees
of toxicity   tell us what we want
to hear & we'll vote for you   honestly

§ 6

peripheral anxieties abound
in tongue-tied acronyms   no more no less
distilling all our wants & needs & who
we are in a few choice syllogisms
bravely said   levelling the playing field
with liars' loans neutron loans ninja loans
all the apparatus of a failed state
in your back pocket   teflon arrangements in
software set to create an icon on
the screen   how do you wish to proceed in
nocturnal parking lots   by taking a
50 % haircut perhaps   with no
regard for body parts   the state withers
but refuses to go away   she read

§ 7

rain matrices the usual routes   knock-off
frocks cut on the bias ultimately
the marketable rendition   firm views
robustly put   wir raten dringend ab
a weapons system failure meant that one
missile did not hit its target   weather
conditions notwithstanding who'd have thought
she saw a bloated water rat floating
in the canal like a pale pin-cushion
a movement at the edge of her vision
magnified by its impending largely
overlooked continuation in the
writers' room discussions of the series
finale with the inevitable

JENNIE OSBORNE

Crow Place

Blackness

wing canopies covering   keeping a lid

glints sharp as nighteyes   sharp as beaks

no fairy-come-follow goldie yammer

We feather-leaf here   incubate

we burrow-root sett here   cubsuckle

Nestraiding loudfoot   thief kill-scent

we tooth against   we claw we

root hole tangle thorn

we nettlebite   stonebreak   soilsmother

Strange enternest   we hatch into earth

rootfood wormfood

all brood all blackness make

Raven

Raven comes dressed as a sleepless night.
He flies away with our sheets.
I watch him go.

Raven comes wearing smiles, spilling out his hurts.
I give him the healing care
I should keep for our bed.

Raven comes dark-feathered, yellow-eyed;
whispers in my ear till I try to steal back
what I have let go.

Neither book nor mirror helps me.
Raven waits, watches me weep,

and when I think he has gone for good
Raven puts on new feathers,
darts in, takes me by surprise.

Sirenum scopuli

The whole island came. Turned
their leather boots
out as rows of ballet men.
No one laughed. They were as cattle
they all lay down before the rain fell.

The circus failed to lock her;
her cherry hair
netted in tents before the woods came.
Silver birch.
She was left to a navy dying. Each sharpened
stone in hand a ticket
which would have paid for breakfast.
Their stomachs rolled by military boots
tying wings of hers
to rocks
to stop her glow.
Sea claimed her thighs. Her stomach.
The children thanked the moon as wolves.

Wives stood over at the hide tide line
sleeves up, dogs
pulling on for nightfall, when
they'd free to fish out liver.

Men adjusted their own
as salt water rose
to choke
the neck of her.
It came to this: one craved
her teeth. Prayed they'd
wash up so he
could thread them on

a checked shirt hem.
Rattle as he walked.

Some bet her wings
would split,
unveiling
shoulder blades.
Waves breaking on a crimson bride.
She did not crack, her bird eyes
blank. If she'd come
with flags they'd have wrapped her in one.
They did not know her colours
just the way she sang.
She opened her mouth then
to catch the feathers.
The men hurled
as they'd been taught as boys.

I heard they gave her a strawberry heart

bred underground. Cured leg meat / bull fighters there to walk
the line. / She came up encased in deepest mud. / She came, then
/ to stand up in a field. / Planted herself. / Her heart pulled up to
the highest branch. / Its green strawberry pulse / pips pushing out
from the inside. / The villagers came. / Their church list brought
/ for Apostles she might answer to. / Her heart hangs. / Pilgrims
came to sit at lunch / to pray for monsoons to wash her clean. /
Scientists wrote / it would take a giant's hand / to reach. / Wives
had timers in their kitchen drawers. / Egg belts across their ageing
stomachs. / Their view the red glow of a farmer's crop. / Their
husbands there with brand new spades. / Break her open as a
chocolate egg. / A blooming girl. / They hung.

Angulimala

Little fingers strung across the door,
festival of you just stopped turning up.
New streak monoxide fixing to inhale
le Peloton speeds towards your rabbit

face the reflection of your own strobe
the possibility of being *la deuxième vie*,
can't make it make a path with a liquorice
Jackhammer. Wheelbarrow: Scene

Two: the problem of unity and the other
Thing. Your bag of poetry wanders off into the
you and me anthology of slightly disingenuous
apologies, the depthless truths of your 'things

men hate about women' and the interminable
tussle over who will wear the encephalogram.

Gift Registry

Drunk, appreciating poetry.
You wonder if *appreciating* poetry
is the same as a velodrome. The heavens
declaiming "it must be sex!"
July fills you with liars

Fancy an overseas trip?

You pick up the wrong pen.
You want to get to the real of him.
But you prefer alcohol.
The Bohemian geometry of open cut crystal.
Counting face.

The Flight of the Temeraire

Three half-skulls of gods speed across the eyes
of canvas, disembodied, they see themselves

As if from the outside

the birth of reflection makes factorial love
to the graphite sea

mathematics bleeds

Next door, it's happening again—

Goodbye Oedipus split into one!
candle masts burned to
                              decent charcoal

oars under cover of the blackless sea,
you number eight—and speed!

Your one doubled up with threes
flays oystered flesh like haggard spumesweet
heads,   enslaved

your kindling awe burned stiff with

                              flight

The Future Lasts a Long Time

Every gulag loves an insomniac
matterhorning the word
for "bowels" in the wrong
place at the right time while
Mistress mouths dictation in
Lourdes or Helsinki until
"we're quite good at it" and "it
feels like licking"

A stamp, senseless, the right name
in the wrong way means "you saw
me coming" and I want you
underground; not sleeping,
dreaming, fingers wishing
for rope, nails humming "a little
something in reserve" in the dirt-

bright room of your natural life.
It is the way we form disaster
starting in on the rim of light
pocketing the darkness of
bodies deep within sound.
Watching your face unseen
I hear the occupation
Of all thoughts singing

what is the use of the song
unsung the river untied
the reasonable doubt of
love's precious means
tickling your wife's slender
throat singing all of our dreams
are about sex except for
the ones that are "about sex".

meet morning

notices	this is where the day could start or stop	forever
taken	as the morning struggles to meet	morning
day	is faced again with reluctant greetings from	one
repeated	to another measured by tone and footsteps	borne
what	in voice and shape—while the cormorant	breaks
design	surface then in seconds dives again—has	breathed
salt	the chill air that you do continuously as	need
need	with no gracefulness and no craving for	salt
breathed	or hot/cold where you have stopped and	design
breaks	your own response to what you see and	what
borne	you don't until too late or often	repeated
one	attempt to begin the journey though the	day
morning	comfort in this freshness is not	taken
forever	granted by you or anyone else who	notices

what you see is not what you get

you hesitate over subtexts then keep walking
there is never any clue in what remains covered

in nature what you see is what you get
you are either quarry or you are not

leads you to think human nature has that angle
that becomes disentangled as you sit in the sun

the lone small wader is difficult to identify
its silhouette on the shore continues regardless

your subtext is an invitation never made
kept at a distance that does not bother the surface

the cliché is that this is just the nature of things
stated by the distant call of a curlew

the ribbed sandbar soon to be covered with water
the place not to visit unless it was already here

a patterned lute

(after Li Shang-Yin 812-858ad)

> The moon is full on the vast sea
> a tear on the pearl
> Li Shang-Yin

i.

it is only accidents in pleasing sounds
that give the lute its strings, its shape, its patterns—
there are patterns that follow each accident
of meeting and parting, tighten or loosen
the strings that hold them to the bridge
that we cross—pluck tunes on the frets—
sound on the air until they are
soundless or until another hears—
or cannot hear because they are not listening
or the sound has become soundless
when the other is ready to hear
or when both make the same sounds when
they are soundless and can only be understood
by sign and the silent patterns of the lute that play on

ii.

it is easy to dream you are a butterfly
that has lost its way and deny the pattern
especially at or before sunrise when the moon
or flickering dawn makes shape vague
even that of Blue Mountain where like
the poem of a haze that emits from fine jade
you are barely able to touch when touched
when touch is like an embrace of seconds
that may need to last for eternity
for there are no sounds spoken or heard—
silent music that celebrates the silent
tick of a great clock watched by both
as its pendulum swings back and forth
as a sign for eyes to see how long this
accident will last, how long it would take
to change the course of a butterfly in a dream

iii.

it is true the lute once had fifty strings—
the White Lady would not, could not stop
a sad tune she continued playing until
Fu-hsi broke the lute in anger
and left her with twenty-five that she
continued to play and can still be heard
for such sounds echo though some may
attempt their silence and break more strings
so those who realise can see and hear—for the oyster
has pearls when the moon is full and the oyster
empty when the evening sky is dark—
such partings are lessened by the paucity
of words that exist to describe them

Eyes

I slip by loss—
consequentially

without doubt
the way a shade lifts

upon the horizon there's a touch—
a fine distinction of gauze

and flowers stare and die
leaving

beginning.

dusk

sum total
I came to the conclusion
of all that I am
of my time not held
was merely some expectation
a solitary sign post
a hankering
as the dusk awaits
and drifts
returning re-discovering
vestiges of confusion
dappled wings

fleeting

I've established an
aptitude a

proficiency

whereby mere capacity
forms logic

the air tonight
rests on a thought
the way
leaves hang on objectivity

while the magpies laugh
bounce

rest me penchant

antipathy

game

Clear sky
words are not
made of this

more than anything
there is instinct

water seems
something different
it falls

or trickles
over rock and
and moss

we are

vicariously experienced
using sympathy
or substitute

we are
end games in oblivion
suggestions

epoch

More

Now
cannot be taken easily
not that eyeshot
of pink
between and simultaneously
almost between
feeling
that bit of grasp/being
a fine distinction
touched in a hint
a shard of light come
darkness

Talk

We like to offer various
forms of illusion

various aspects of norm

as this willow here bends reeds
to drink

words come to me
like pillow talk/contusion

Hear it ! I'm right
you're wrong

there are so many ways of being
chameleons know this

or ghosts

it's like a deafening racket
that hits excreta

a wind fan of urine

insanity votes

The Mind's Weather

As if a weathercock could uproot a house,
as if within his eye

which turns and chimes upon each unweighted thing
he held the knack for telekinetics.

His pivot rests above me,
neck over neck,

and I under his rooftop make do
with brow-wrinkled maps.

He loves what he cannot move, cattle like rocks
on the corners of the world's tarpaulin.

His balance requires unfailing concentration.
With a twist

he hauls a net of silver-stomached
gales over one shoulder.

And though a mind like mine
might reduce him to wire, coat-hanger bird,

his jurisdiction extends
to the hill's diaphragm, which heaves to his inspection.

He is the centrepoint
to the land's scales, herding rain

to a lake eastward
to ballast swallows bent on migration.

His brain is magnetic,
my breath is iron filings.

Impossible, how he directed his arrow downwards,

summoned a fimbulwinter
with motionless wings,

and I in the basement
with a single candle,

hearing the rooftiles diverge
and fall like fledglings.

Ghost

It had a pulse, the rhythm of a blinking eye.
Its breath blew over one's face.
It sat in the aviary and all the birds had flown.

When they came with callipers they could not measure it.
Now starved, now glutted, it broke them apart
and their distance hung in the air.

A thrown bucket of sand discerned its shape
but the sand was mute
and could think only of glass.

It had eyes, possessing whatever looked upon it
and whatever mouths answered did so only for themselves.

It sat in the tigers' enclosure
and peeled away the rinds to reveal their coal bodies.
It flickered like a candle suckling on the air.

Within a Budding Grove

It is simple enough: all windows
tarry this aspect
and even at such close distance.

Lay a stone here, then
step back
into descant and day.

True, I have fallen more than
once getting here,
eyes trained on other corners.

An attitude of seams, spacing
this ground
and all manner of convergences.

Whole cities might be made from
this, sloughs of colour,
all information and humming.

Through the woods a young boy comes,
arms of etchings
and deep pockets pitted with bark.

So it is hands harvest holding
and are taken back,
frequently, to fell, clough, and pike.

And then to stand, brackish and estuarine,
at that precise point
where the crossing happens.

Peripheral Vision

> some kind of immaculate decision
> just let it out as it is
> a book instead of a ring

Something you do, a way of focussing, of registering an object, an other's body, the line of cheek-bone, jut of jaw. To stand in a mirror as four pupil-discs, frame and prune of iris, and map vertigo with a rake. To measure the mould of motion, the precise time and space of particle and ellipsis, brow waves, strip of floorboard, skin. The angle-flow of elbow, entangle.

> handfuls of silver letters handmade for the service
> and we promised on a Saturday
> though Fridays cheaper and catering fish

All night the well-rushing melt of your knee in my chest, clambering sides. What happens to pronouns when we sleep? By morning I give you a book bound in hide, a little water-stained and marked by someone else's hand. Everywhere letters intend you and I. Out of the window the weather descends upon itself, wrapped in skein and canal, a flock of wild geese in pattern and flight.

> the clothes we wore
> linen and so traditionally thin
> and the day all wind and brittle

Imperceptibly this is still what it is. So it is space is edifying and number cannot properly be held to ground just as the measure of letters is not so much one of occurrence but more the curve of what typographers carve and carry, working in shifts, too hot for the pressing. It is slow labour and often there are false starts and mistakes but even sheet metal, it seems, may compact into I love you.

> two weeks to merry
> then from pier to trawler rousing the sea
> for family wage and home

Not easy to be what you say, a geometric plane of sound vowels lost in air of derivation. Matter, it seems, must tow line, although convergence too is also the edge of letting go. The point of flight, I am told, is its own body, tendon-tissue bent to the inter-course of palms while peripheral vision, simply, is occupied with the roundness of corners and the sliding of profiles.

> even now when it is cold
> I do not wear a hat
> afraid of what it might do to my remaining hair.

If Any Oarsman Should Hear My Voice

> Are you
> afraid
> of dying?
>
> said the little
> boy who spoke
> to Jesus.
>
> Why do you ask?
> I said.
> Because your eyes,
>
> he said,
> are water
> without footprints.
>
> Soon after
> the little boy
> stood at the bow,
>
> stretched
> and drilled holes
> in the helm.

Lynne Hjelmgaard

The Other Boat

(off South France's Gulf of Lion)

In the throws of a Tramontare I spy another boat
surf erratically down the heightened slope of a wave.

Pellets of rain hit rippling swells, lethal bullets
on the surface, and dissolve. Freakishly, the skipper

on the other boat attempts to motor against the seas.
No storm sail is hoisted for ballast.

She is a toy, a flimsy teacup in boiling stew for the sea-beast,
and eerily disappears from sight.

We are in the Lion's mouth, territory unknown,
it speaks as if to say:

I too long for the smell and comfort of land
and want to leave once it's tasted.

It is better to sit above, secured with a harness if you're rested
and dry. The plunging motion in the belly of the vessel is a strain.

When I saw the other boat I stared blankly until it didn't exist
Now I am content just to be warm.

Annalise rides the top of a crest, her bow points precariously downwards
until loyally and steadily at the last moment
she lifts.

And we can log the miles.

CrissCross

The voyage is a past you needed
to catch up with. A congruent line.

The months since the journey moved
in their own latitudes and longitudes

crisscrossed with colour and weather
to harden your face.

A storm: you stay in the middle of things
I head for the bunk.

I remember waves like fountains etched on paper.
We rounded the point longing for harbour.

The blue wind, the biting spray.
The relentless sea shoving us from side to side.

Still you thrive in an ocean's wild night
and spike your coffee with too much rum.

The problems arrive post-Atlantic
and must be solved on shore.

Now you blame the both of you:
the one with the mad eyes and briefcase
the other for the sea story he holds.

ROBERT VAS DIAS

Episode

Getting up, unsteady, the me
       in the mirror is not the me

who keeps my memories,
       who wears the face, familiar

but odd, an oblong look
       into those eyes I seem

never to have seen.
       The slate's clean: how to begin

again, how regain, claim family,
       friends, where this room, where

the city, people I can call
       my own, anyone I can call for help?

Look deep into the eyes: they
       have seen where my life has gone.

"So how was your trip?"

You knew or assumed
    the worst but let me
        assure you—sending

that little gleam of
    schadenfreude underneath
        your feigned anticipation—

that everything went smoothly
    train dead
        on tie, no motion

sickness, lurching or
    snuffling dogs, no
        snivelling people arguing

with the conductor over
    paying, no smoking, eating
        pungent food, vomiting

the heating reasonably
    for once, adjusted, altogether
        comfortable it must be

said, though my wish
    of getting to where
        I'd like to be—

interesting to you
    in my coming, or going—
        has come to nothing.

The Fetch

This particular wind has blown a long way over open water. Dipping down like a bird or swirling up out of sight, but mostly held tight to the tops of numerous waves, at once urging and holding on for life.

A distance I've travelled. Between continents, across years. Land mass after land mass, hillock and cliff, shore and flowering wood—all could have stopped me. Should have, perhaps.

Today is frighteningly brisk. It wouldn't take much to tear a sail, collapse some stones. Let go the rope. I'm so tired, now that I think about it, of keeping us afloat.

Perfect Summer's Day 1

At a certain point, the sun and clear blue sky and turquoise sea wipe the slate clean. You notice instead the ways gulls chase, two on two, unsettling each other like relay runners, passing an invisible baton: your turn now to fly low, test good weather and calm water. Together you pass over, descend, move along the shore, your wings in unison, bare centimetres from a splash, crash and headlong fall.

Despite the dangers you hold onto your hard-won momentum, stay in the race.

Perfect Summer's Day 2

For a moment I'm thinking anything is possible. I can run
and my knees won't give way. You could phone and sound the
same. I won't burn in this sun, and everyone here is in love.

And to step on water is to step on land. To glide on one is to
slide along the other. There is no shingle, no failure to reach
the horizon, no treading water, no going under, no running
to catch up, no giving in, no heartbreak and no letting go.

Little Blue Hut

Another clear morning in high wind. At home you've left
cats warming and rolling on the drive, the lime green of
new-leaved trees, fragile pink of apple blooms.

Overhead now, a dozen gulls circle, riding something,
searching, saying something or nothing. White as clouds in
the cloudless sky, they somehow lead you.

Here you have come to expect the unexpected. To abandon
plans. Look elsewhere for dependable weather.

Day after day the wind blows in. And you press further
and further out from your wooden house, tip seaward
with no rudder and no soil to hold you. Only air speeds,
tides and currents, temperatures and moisture to go by.
The mysterious, unfixed sky, these shifting waters, endless
hidden gradients of land.

Structure

When my mother was driving back and forth in between the homes of husband A and husband B, what do you think she did in the interim? If you, iris/irises were at the helm, how would the world adapt to suit your—not your need—but your longings? Architectural harmony, says. Arch of tones, says. Bridge bridge bridge, says. Sunset-peace, says. Sunrise-joy, says. Heaven and earth, says. Everything else, says. If I wished the world to be well, it would be well. My bare arms would appear with fists of flowers. Trumpeting petals. A burst iris so that I could come down for breakfast. Buried in the dark earth, the end of our suffering.

Then that which you fear was over. It ended abruptly. The irises bent a little. There are passages to and from other worlds.

Uses

Well, she longed, and she knew not what for. Had the world nothing she might live to care for? Loved her own harmless gifts. Saying, unsaddened, this shall soon be faded. Who shall never name thee. My mother was three-fold in nature, like a flashing falcon in her daring, and had three husbands. My mother was a florist. Many pursued her with fire, and some with envy. She was often in a careful mood, but I don't know if this mood is what caused so many to pursue her, or the result of it. The third husband (husband C) had a name that was too long to tell. He was a man like a slender sapling. She told me: he bedded me in awful thistle and vile nettles full of vice. But on the day we wed, he was dressed in fringe and a vest with many dashes, and I scattered gold spots in its open breast.

When we walked among the irises she said, "I know that these pure waters and Flags know me, as my dogs know me. And I cannot change my name, you see. Like a strictly botanical name, my name is hard to change, especially a name expressing such obvious characteristics." This conversation could not have taken place elsewhere. "For a start, we would have to change the basis of the present universally accepted binomial nomenclature. No more homo sapiens. No more knife and fork."

Care

I find five irises, and call them lovely. I'd like to investigate. We drift hand in hand through a hall... painted like a fresh prow... Do[es] your root drag up color? I can smell the gorgeous bogend with fire on your cheeks and brow. A man renounces the entire world—clothes, money, a job, a woman, daily breakfast, contact with friends, flesh & intimacy, flesh & books, what he thinks he knows—so that he can travel into the center of an iris. This is like having access to the tongue itself. Or the Law of mountains and lakes. One[s] become mountains and lakes through merit. But addressing the iris, he says: stained with your cool violet, I observe you and therefore, I change you. Am I rewriting your future
purple drop-
loped tongue-
splayed shooting-
star kingplant?
["Am I rewriting your future purple drop-loped tongue-splayed shooting-star kingplant?"]
Have I heard you yet, and what is it the people want to hear?
[What is it you want to say to the people?] [also given that they are narrowing?]

As a starting place, return to your stalks."

more meanderings

I had met her feeding pigeons from a tesco bag
her hair dishevelled with mist before spring
it was outside gresham college by the wrought iron gate

I spoke about lectures there   baudelaire's journey
to mauritius   Iain sinclair who would lecture
on rivers tonight   but she had never been
to one   I was glad about that somehow
told her instead of a blossom tree in the inner square
a little mouse at its base I had photographed
she smiled   looked in her bag for a last crust
I told her about rats that used to swim the river
then turned to catch the tube at chancery lane
thinking of tunnels dusty mice in the underground
wished to say no more but she tugged at

my sleeve *let's go to the blossom tree*
I showed her the hidden courtyard   we sat in the
late sun   listened to wandering footsteps   the call
of birds waited for the swish of a tail
she forgot I was there

ruins support the weight of the city

roman fort & city wall 200 AD
poppies & graces inhabit stones
buddleia in cracks
cement footbridge

plaque reads
boundary of the parish of st. botolphs
extended 9 feet southward
of this wall
messages throughout the week
a church building has stood here
for nearly 1000 years
proclaiming death & resurrection

religious houses dot
street patterns

guild church of
st mary aldermary standing 900 years
cooks hall destroyed 1771

the aldergate
has talks every tuesday
the site of the meeting place of
rev. john Wesley

within the city wall was safety
it being a defensive barrier

london grew beyond the wall

NICHOLAS YB WONG

Katia Kapovich's Face/Book

What's the occasion tonight? You're wearing
melancholy, not makeup, in this B/W book jacket shot.
The background trees, your denim blazer,
equally bedimmed, neither earns more
nostalgia. A cigarette—unlit—between your first
& middle fingers that tap only on paper
scraps & studs: a mnemonic device for your
tobacco aura. Your head lowers, eyes downcast,
you shimmy home, or a place fuzzier—
a second home maybe. But what have we learnt
about homes except they're where
photos abound? I thank optical fibers
for connecting me with your auburn hair, & you—
wholly colored—though much sadder.
The cigarette's still there, lit but smokeless.
Your eyes, this time, look askance into the lens,
as if you found, behind the machine, your image,
your double, subcutaneous self. I hesitate—
I'm tempted to befriend you in this dimension
where distance doesn't exist, but your pale skin
& gray eye circles object, your personal profile's set
quasi-private, an inelastic border with the public.
So I leave you alone, better remain a stranger to you
& you to me. Let's face the present, let's draw
a mental line. The way solitude is earned, such simple.

Carnivore

The best way to rid an addiction
is to get addicted to something else.
That's why my father hopped from gin
to ginger juice, from pork chops to plums
(which help his metabolism)
& from women to woman. He welcomes
his 70th birthday by sitting on the couch,
with a cup of warm oolong tea,
watching a grainy Shaw Brothers film
about blind swordsmanship.

They say when one gets old, birthdays
mean nothing, but nothing's been said
if the other 364 days relatively mean
any less. Since he stops seeing
his birthday as an event, I stop buying gifts.
I ask from him instead. What a filial son. I say
I can afford a bathtub, but not the space
that accommodates one. I say *sell*
your house, get a smaller one. I wish
to say *I need the rest as down payment*
for my own selfdom, freedom, fleeting—

His eyes stay on the TV, as if it's experiential
to watch blind warriors wrangling. But they're actors,
paid to lose their sight at the set.
My father knows this, though he's not moving
in front of those vintage images,
like a cold-blooded crocodile in dark water,
saving residual energy, against
changes that turn him into a prey.

Rob A. Mackenzie

from **Nocturnes**

III

a beautiful busker calls
"…you're my wonderwall"

    or perhaps   wallflower
                Windy Miller
                winterwilly stroking
                    the shores of Lake Windermere

      no mind
    or obvious wonder

        for one night only
      midnight's smoking jacket slowly
                unbuttoning

        nightmare loop
    Margaret Thatcher jiggling on top
      shouting, "No milk for you!"

  still working the 27th floor
city boys gamble
    someone else's life
      and lose

  the usual novelties
    repeat themselves

      a helicopter leap is the new
    marriage registry office
        parachute
    or no parachute
        morning will fall

V.

evening service

    fawnsuit with glasses and ruby earring
                looms from the vestibule

tightless girls
    cold-shoulder the drifting organ

      who needs ecstasy when
          the wayside pulpit
          the open-windowed Jag
                provide, provide
    "gonna be OK, just…"

      dance past the posters girls

come to our toy library
    come to our coffee morning
      come to your zumba keep-fit

      dole out the hymnbooks fawnsuit
the choir puff their cushions
    endorse peppermint air

      and someone will improvise a prayer
    if you party
though that door

    or with bottles waving arches
               queues outside
    the endangered public toilet
below *Happy Holidays* in neon

      check those nose-rings!
        extemporise fawnsuit
    on fleshy thorns
    on pierced skin

scarlet lippy round the pews

fawnsuit pours Ribena into a goblet
"the blood of Christ"
            for bodies soft as bread

Lynx mob vs. Brut gang
neo-Calvinist peashooters
humanist bollocks

                to celebrate 'winterfest'
        obliterate consciousness

add meaning
        stripped down
            to the least offensive point

                        a continuous period
            extended ellipsis

6 Haiku

keeping out the rain
a famous part of Paris
before the Eiffel Tower

*

falling leaves
down the garden path
the distance in light years hasn't changed

*

the side street's lower speed limit
—
a few trees changing
color

*

last minute cancelled reservations
the rives continues
to bend

*

one color sky
boxes of new shoes
out of fashion

*

the foot of the mountain
the stars make us
wait

"The Garden of Eden"

nothing other than arm
        as bare as mine—nothing varied,
        as unalterable.

        one sound that set us apart—
        on one side—from other sounds.

        there lavender spreads out its annulets.
        we enter the right to abolish
        the volute motions of time :

an arm as bare as ours
        spheres around.
        what collects within the curve
        we knead with flour, seed and oil

        the bare of our arms
        doughs forth the light.

Autumnal

Sadness prevails.   no longer
an anguish
nor a corkscrew
mentioned rapidly into the marrow

a felt
clothing off the internal borders
between the dusk and the following
resurrectional morning.

for long
crows' sparse names

will remain unevoked.
                    Sadness
retains its humid
throughout the season; our lips endure,
hands sustain on the milk we are
to warm over and over.

Untitled

We are shreds forgiven
blessed set at naught

via the side lane of a thousand years
a vicarious pardon comes
takes a seat
on the side
orchestrates our blood currents our
invisible intersections

invites us to happen
(the rhythm of tango and other
selected forms of the sleepless)

our private mornings
follow us closely,
we listen inside
to the dot-and-dash messages
sent through the septum.

At night
we coincide, and
rewind the clock winter-wise

and build a city
upon this city
from our raw material.

Untitled

It is time to start being
towards winter. To sift apart marbles
and broken marbles,
their dry sounds' prefiguration of dawnless pilgrimage
into the rooms. The season of ribs and invisible crows.

at 5 p.m. to brew a subtime
of the late oils and brown bitter
apophthegmatic roots of an ash tree. Time to
cloth over the spoken
from the behind-faces.
To leave the knots undo their knots.

Untitled

My riverman, our green comes

from the bottommost corners, we are

vitally sombre and ever-safe

with our barrels and arms

unloaded, inoculated against rust,

midnight navigation, syllables borne upon

the upper layers of water, all counter-spells and mast-

-bound mariners,

their sharp edges and corrugated shells

of their astray-gone years.

PAULA KONEAZNY

Devotee of Birds

> thinking about Rachel Carson
> *Are you my mother?/ Said the baby bird to the bulldozer—*
> Claudia Keelan ('Little Elegy (Eros)')

for there to be an elegy, first there has to be a someone

stepping out of sight　　　engaged in close examination of

the blissful matter-of-fact

a still photographer / still, a photographer

I wait to see who'll come by

sometimes glancing at the drifting

halation around "This is where I came in."

her reputation for precision　　jostled by

streaks of life curveting

sound ballooning　　above　　under　　and through　　her feet

I take her likeness with a periscope

in the meantime / word's depiction

its rhythmic lashing

*　　　　　you can sing it*

migration-fever streams through the perforations

(no carefree love)   sucked into mouths

cilia setting off an undercurrent

the photograph should not be so alluring

as to spin the historical record

let's talk about dollars

> *off the hook*

sensitive lateral lines   appear as facts   waiting to be taken

luring the fishes to rise   and seize the deep beaches

never to stray to the wrong continent for a meal

the photograph must be radically destabilized

before it can be reintroduced

back-to-back exposures occur : method of take

captive breeding can't reproduce

integrity, the lonely possibility, is an impulse

to become one of the local browsing names

not to disturb the un-emptiness of the place

shells in their clutches

ammunition zone

seen by birds or

> *listened to by birds*

The Whole River & All of the Land

If you think you're alone / You haven't learned the language
          —Brenda Hillman ('Hydrology of California')

I like her on airplanes / on the steps of capitols
& on park benches in international locations
poem in her lap / like Mary Austin's "perfected and depleted flower"

because she has the poem / it has to go somewhere
that's how this works / by saying

          water travels great distances to quench our thirst

the *we* in weather builds dams / it seems / just for fun
passes Go on a sliding current / sips directly from the water table

vibrations created by Manifest Destiny cause clouds to form

rain keeps falling & falling & falling / nitric acid & sulfuric acid
with their acquisitive "c"s / hungry little creatures / made entirely of
appetite

countershading / once separated from the body / with its complicated
aquatics

rain's shadow captures most of the energy / acquires acuity
in the ecotone / where always ended a long time ago

          *we do not know how to grow big trees**

in the name of the estero / and of the slough / and of the lands
which are are all of the lands

beaver & prairie dog implicate / the amount of water
a poem can hold / disturbed forests in the drinking water
completely lack lungs / we breathe through their skins

          *Alice Outwater *(Water: A Natural History)*

Camilla Nelson

wrIting apple

finger writer finger   holder   scar holder cackcrackling joint jagged
frazz of apple teeth   meat   meet apple
here,   unidentified   onset
now I'm not myself   nor you   either
in its not self mine   inset   decay's unrepresentable
hard peaks of wrinkled skin   will I soon become
like this   my cheeks' blush   brown decay
what horror   lies in earth   hold still,
let me examine   your fine lines of teeth
your skin   raised creviced lines   wrinkles I gave   you
gave me these wrinkles   oh my words   let me examine you
examine yours and mine together what is their difference their identity
effect oh mine   oh yours   oh mine and yours together in a prayer of
        wrinklings
in my writing with you   fleck   your skin   I say you thought some
        object because
you other than   you addressee   you dressed   undressed
in writing   of a sudden   lingo-d out of   life in terminology   form
of knowledge far from appling   sapling, old and fruitless   all written
        over now with
words from   world that is,   human   mindful,   mind full
no brain you   respond   yes   this is what you are   writing   telling
        read my
write my   you affecting me affecting you affecting me affecting
stopping   no full stopping

83

from Written Responses
to Photographs and Audio Recordings,
Reading and Writing with a Tree 2010–2012

(10:30am 6th Jan 2011 response to audio recorded on same day
@ 08:30am 6th Jan 2011)

*the sound of grass under me   squelch of inarticulate mutterings
resistant to bearing a body   brunt of rain, grass   precision of camera
framing   jars with soluble experience the sufferance such weather means
breath   huff   click of rain nails   static impatient with environmental
facts & wishing myself out of this discomfort   rain-like ice of fingers ear
full of what my skin wants not to listen to   the cold   unwilling part in
drowning vision   orchard awkward   sharpness on my skin   almost at
sea in the greens of moss and lichen and the pale green grass and the hard
snap of rain*

reader write a response

melting glass to needle point   become the lichen sponge

sound overwhelms   of tree on rain and road on rain and head

and hair on paper audio   speaking rain

the crackle of a gramophone   algen fungae grown together

rain confused words   dictaphone is glockenspiel

rain, jewels on wire necklace   the absent speech of thought

between speeds   putting leaves to bed

reader write a response

so loud   the expectation of rain   the violence of water

unobliterate   continuum   lip stiff   flat throat   mutterer

don't let her in   screaming gulls mew   loudmouthed

thought in rain   it be whatever you want it to be

desire, the great transformer   swish unhappy swipe of waterproof
rubbing rain towards skin   eventual   invasion
listen to those legion armies   hear their will   to touch your skin
         the softness of beauty,   the hard ache of rain

reader write a response

what is the shape of this leaf-drenched feeling
rain fall sounds of trapped wings   on a window
somewhere other than   this   what   is my familiar
in what language tree names rain   a scrawl I can't quite read
but feel to mean

reader write a response

the parrot squeak of camera tongue   needs flash to see   (darkener)
automatic bird   each wing flap opens eye   and mouth at once
mew to see   swallow up a square of this   and store it flat
in undeveloped meaning

reader write a response

only intonation   meaning sound is wordless
phrasing with the shape of mouth   lip   throat   teeth   tongue
chorus with the brain to furnish noise with sense   but all I hear
is human bird song   word blur   sound taps through you
breath emitting organ sound beyond   breath sound body
earth sound water

Water Coins

faced twice,
air-spin dance song's
luck, & to chance all the
marrow, though if what picks
gold in the vein

bones cloud from
sun-flesh, reflects the true
points, & wells tears, lies flat
down, the tale's lost, sunk
in rain-slime

& where glint
quarrels the surface, not
going deeper, our dark wound's
unseen, yet disturbs, a scum dis-
charging sleep.

what will keep
is this well drawn water:
its circles' bright now, not wishes
falling, just a tender trade,
or love of light

Connect

Room

without the spur
   there's no touch
to the source
   & no switch-
ing to light;
  silence is
   deep, as if
submarine,
   & sounding
the room's shape;
   the curtain's
sigh, the creak
of depthless
   floor, the cord's
faint tap on
   the wall: there's
no outlet—
  or mouse in
the wainscot;
   never the
smallest noise
of this now
   circuiting;
inside, wind-
   owless breath:
only the whisper
  of what's fur-
ther than gal-
   axies, spurred
through the night.

Spurs

   the day: cross
-stitching rain,
   leaf spirals
down, though
   each island's
  soft-cliff grey
is a cloud
   —beach fringe white,
& somehow
  light, beyond
the weather
    *

  sky gravel
walk, silence
   between what
steps closer;
& thin legs
forking, the
  arthritic
crack of the
   light giant: thin
bone-flash nar-
rows the count
    *

Apollo
gone with the
  Lamb, fleece
soiled when west-
  ering with
   modern gods:
   the forms of
red, though it's
   what hides in
the black sings,
   rewiring stars

from Earthly Strain & Mare's Tails

earthly strain

singing to the ghost
  & not a chord
enchanting in the
  the aether
even the highest
  note's no sound
in the upper air:
  the fifth element,
where Gods breathe
   what we cannot;
  yet since there is
no luminferous
bridge, however
  the soul urges,
all that we bring is
   the impure song
   tearing the voice
    diminished, but
     now—& here.

dispersal

explaining
sundogs mocks
all old gods
Apollo in green
& blue
  old storm
  gatherer
  gone, mourning
  for his glory;
nephology &
the rainbow fire:
  a precise
  discourse
  of haze &
  colour-
why
  never again
  the union of
cloud & man
that left the
centaur-tracks
to trail across
    the sky

Measure

from pitch
back to its original

quiet tangle
of birchbark.

Down along
the frost encased

river, little
stinging reeds

thresh muscle
endlessly, stricken

to worry and ruffle
surfaces like this.

Enormous funnels
of pitch a people

press on, tamp
the thicket's

thickset quiet out
as if a current

of flame rouses
deep under boats

pitch-sealed
to carry them over.

Without an usher
or single familiar

landmark yet
the pilgrim

entering woods
hears pitch drip

from the sphere
of fixed stars.

The Work

ichorous tissue
cooling nude

on the bone
in this sieve

we achieve
transparency

reading fluent
from news

and weather a
sudden rose's

snaked-off skin
the glass apple

a crushed
and humble light

onyx preserves
makes possible
whose core
is ark air

Having been permitted

to wander
the ante-
pasture

lately bare
of
foxglove's

pretext
snow

gnawed down
to ascetic

thirst, I scan

the stillness here
for a certain defect

on the surface
a procession

of children
might have left

that their games
be counted
in memory

despite
having been
on all sides

flanked by ice
until

what's empty
no longer
serves

discipline but

calves a wailing
multitude:

words

not-made-
by-hands

that won't touch
what hands

cannot

not knowing
their own
print yet, how

ice is known

to give way
by the arrival

of hallowed
grasses

Capability Procedures

1

Changed by observation:
not cat more. The pressure
risen on the bell, portholes
thicken with the soupy air,
he moves—an astronaut
blown to slow ridiculous,
a puffy suit of questions.

*

Each leaf its own torn
shadow that spills volume
to the ground. The very wait
a kind of lightness. Trills
inflected on the grass, bare
breeze, the neuropathic flinch
of blades. Say something once.

*

Abstract
telephonic tact:
a neutral act
acts natural
as 'background facts'.
Patter.
Lack.

2

Ground down these grains
must all be graded.
The objective is the name
we give the little lens
of the toy telescope,
all far-away-and-wee
as that finer flower.

*

Where the buck stops he smells
the air. From here the slowing
frames blend and the mind's
CGI churns over, violets
balletic on fresh grass. The kill
is here, only not yet. Patience.
Brick by brick they build a trap.

*

To: Re: cc:
FW: Re:
To: Bc   c:
Re: Fw:
Cc: Bcc: Re:
Fw:
Recall this message

3

The wrangler locks the ride.
Break the plastic curtain as you will
the glass wall holds. Support
cold metal as the fake lights
blare and derivative

acceleration jounces out
on little tracks. Not frightened. Tired.

*

Backwards on each hoofprint,
every scuff and broken twig
appeals the origin. The forest
alive with sin and forgiving,
where each cast is perfect
evidence, angle, umbra:
the step from the path.

*

The bored
cries under pressure,
the bolder
rolled already
down the hill:
the Venus Fish Bar.
Brillo. Steel.

4

Energy saving bulb i' th'earth,
more corm, drilled above death
every season, why wake up?
Why not wake down? The down
-wake of the off-bound ferry
turning the bags of history
for the gulls. Equal and opposite.

Forty watt: to think we volunteered.

*

The bone
undertow
where he is turned
white
chimes to charm
the current
in the dark.
Thy Father

language struck
will not
un-ring.

5

The forest is a maze
where our design leads
us away or comes out to
the cliffs of light. Exposed
upon the brick of outcome:
Promethean (except his liver
has a daily respite—nightly
eaten).

*

Hears pewits worry tone
over the marsh. Everywhere
the acrobats dispute
indistinguishable
land or half-land. The drains
will be abandoned and let it
all in, all out, let it.
Tide.
Bells ever further into the water.

*

With delicate logic
woodland treads
a net for all
the flowers. Too many
reasons do not rest.
Golfers call it
the yips. And still
the small feet
running
running as accustomed.

6

The substance alters
but the colours stay
the same: Victorian,
a small beer and tobacco
brown, plastic tribute
to the second quality
of glass, empty
and full of history,
that placebo pull.

*

As the window bars
the retina, so inner
sight is bleach-marked
and will distress the sliding
world until matched
on memory. The brand
is permanent. The bruised
mirror of the eye
protects its killer.

7

Trees lay out a language
on the grass in grisaille.
It replies (quite crudely) "GREEN"
that one thing at least.
All the dance of folding
crushed to plain.
A traffic accident.

*

Outside the skin the sea
begins. These squamous bricks
still watery and shed
like shadows that imagine
joining. Pretended
battle lines. Admission
as our best defence.

Waves for Mike Taylor
(pianist, drowned by own hand, 1969)

but don't you all   sometimes   wish to disappear
I've been waiting ages for this bus   Sorry Not In Service

sometimes it wanders off and the fingers   do their own thing
wander the shoreline of a badly-tuned piano

don't you want to walk on the water

it won't stay in tune without attention   thoughts
return to the theme of a road around and a road across

in my dreams invent the myth of an island   don't we all
want to swim to a landfall   sooner or later

repeat to fade   take up thy bed of notes and walk
gently washed ashore   unrecognisable   metrical

untidy tides   listen to the keys you don't play

blue notes rise from below   or is it just me
sick of my own company   voice drowned in each

musical phrase   see the geese fly home   just add water

to feel what hunger feels   each chord a remembrance
further up the shore than the one before

everyone will miss us   then they'll see

whatever you throw in the sea   where giants live
returns changed   out of all   cognition

The Local

                    her varying subject matter
what's a little rain
                    creamy Victorian market hall
of its shoe leather
                    hide your thoughts close
you preferred your own company
                              Miners Arms Sacred Heart
even good typists make errors
                         no worse there is none
in that demolished space
                         not eating enough losing the thread
appeal for the Pals' memorial
                         between dark and light
candour you'd rather we forgot
                         the bus stammers out
the kind of rain that soaks

                    as a short-sighted private
but you never visit
                    and don't come back
clouds drop low on the hills
                         who died on the wires and
you should have been there
                         hung there one of two
two more holes in the road
                         the scrubbed and washed estate
become a thin place
                         wives locked in marriage
forgets where it put itself
                         the harmonics of the poetic
the memorial to the fallen
                         quiet and simple
the kind of rain that soaks

                                    because you never stay
return please to Manchester
                          by the hole in the middle
rain sluicing down
                    avant-garde despite itself
last night's fireworks tater pie
                              youth's whiny voice
the old man's complaint
                        blank space and brick dust
weren't you the mardy get
                          and a long list of names
a unique waterside view
                          this kind of intense
chance encounters at work
                              the local rag
the kind of rain that soaks

The Vampire

Sudden as the stab of a knife,
you lodged yourself in my sad heart.
Like a horde of demons running rife,
you flaunt your folly, tarted out,

treating me like your unmade bed.
You've made my spirit your domain,
you infamous bitch—I'm bound and tied
to you as the convict is to his chain,

as the drunkard is to his cheap red,
as the stubborn gambler to the game,
as carrion comfort to the worm.
I call down curses on your head!

I've begged the quick blade of the sword
to win me back my liberty,
I've had a word with cyanide—
"Aid me in my infirmity!"

No use. The poison and the sword
contemptuously answered me:
"You worthless fool, as if we would!
There's no route out of slavery,

you're marked in red on all her maps.
Besides, our help would be in vain,
you'd fall to kissing her again
and bring to life her vampire corpse."

Correspondences

In Nature's temple, eerie words and cries
escape their living pillars and arcades;
a thousand symbols breathe in woods and glades,
and watch us pass, with long-familiar eyes.

The way far-distant echoes spread and blend
into a deep and shadowy unity
vast as the night or daylight clarity,
perfumes, sounds and colours correspond.

Some scents are delicate as children's flesh,
gentle as oboes, green as meadow grass,
others are corrupt, triumphant, lush,

seeming infinite things as they diffuse—
incense, storax, musk and ambergris
sing out the soul's delight, the body's bliss.

The Abyss

Pascal's abyss went everywhere with him.
—But it's all abyss—action, word, dream,
desire! Time and again, the icy wind
of abject fear has set my hair on end.

Above, below, all round, the chasms wait,
the utter quiet, the lure and terror of space . . .
God's knowing finger draws along the base
of hydra-headed dark a nightmare state.

I shrink away from sleep, a gaping hole
full of faceless horror's endless fall;
at any window . . . just infinity.

I'm haunted by such vertigo and dread,
I envy the unfeeling, senseless void.
—Will forms and numbers never let me be?

The Rebel

An angry angel swoops like a hawk on his prey,
grabs the wretched fellow's hair in his fist
and shakes him fiercely: "Listen to what I say!
I'm your good angel, right? And I insist

you have to love them all (stop those grimaces),
the bad, the dull, the crippled and the poor—
that red carpet for the coming of Jesus
is made of charity, which is your chore.

Such is love! So while your heart can feel,
to the greater glory of God, refuel your zeal,
the true delight that never dies away."

Chastisement equals charity it seems—
the giant fist pounding the damned, who screams
over and over, "No, I won't. No way!"

Evening Harmony

Each stem is trembling with the turning year
as all the flowers, like censers, breathe and pulse.
With languorous vertigo, a plaintive waltz,
sounds and perfumes swirl in the evening air.

All the flowers, like censers, breathe and pulse;
the shuddering violin is a heart laid bare;
sounds and perfumes swirl in the evening air.
The clear sad sky's an altar and resting-place.

The shuddering violin is a heart laid bare,
a tender heart that dreads the black abyss.
The clear sad sky's an altar and resting-place:
in thick blood-light, the sun is drowning there . . .

A tender heart that dreads the black abyss
guards every scrap the shining past will spare;
the sun, in thick blood-light, is drowning there . . .
Your memory glows in me like the Eucharist!

NOTES ON CONTRIBUTORS

AMANDA ACKERMAN lives in Los Angeles where she is co-editor of the press, eohippus labs. She has a book *The Seasons Cemented (Hex Presse)* and the forthcoming *I Fell in Love with a Monster Truck* (Insert Press).

CHARLES BAUDELAIRE (1821–1867) should need no introduction. The poems here are drawn from his famous collection, *Les Fleurs du mal* (1857).

JAMES BELL has two collections from Tall Lighthouse, most recently *fishing for beginners* (2010). He lives in Brittany.

MELISSA BUCKHEIT'S *Noctilucent* appeared from Shearsman in March.

JEN CAMPBELL is a writer and bookseller living in London. Her poetry has recently appeared in *The Rialto, Poetry London* and *Agenda*, and her first book: *Weird Things Customers Say in Bookshops* was published by Constable and Robinson. Her blog is at jen-campbell.blogspot.com.

MARTYN CRUCEFIX has published five collections, most recently *Hurt* (Enitharmon, 2010). His translation of Rilke's *Duino Elegies* (Enitharmon, 2006) was shortlisted for the Popescu Translation Prize.

PATRICIA DEBNEY teaches at the University of Kent. Her first collection of prose poems, *How to Be a Dragonfly* (Smith Doorstop), was the overall winner of the 2004 Poetry Business Book and Pamphlet Competition.

NIKOLAI DUFFY is a lecturer at Manchester Metropolitan University. His chapbook, *the little shed of various lamps*, is from The Red Ceilings Press.

CARRIE ETTER is the author of *Divining for Starters* (Shearsman, 2011) and *The Tethers* (Seren, 2009), and also edited the Shearsman anthology *Infinite Difference* (2010). She teaches at Bath Spa University.

CATHERINE HALES lives in Berlin. Shearsman published her first collection, *hazard or fall*, and her translations of Norbert Hummelt in 2010.

FIONA HILE has poetry published or forthcoming in *The Age, The Sun-Herald, Southerly, Hecate, Steamer* and *Rabbit*. She is currently completing a PhD in creative writing at The University of Melbourne.

LYNNE HJELMGAARD'S latest book is *The Ring* (Shearsman, 2011)

GARY HOTHAM lives in Maryland. In 2010, Pinyon Publishing (Montrose, CO), published a major collection of his work: *Spilled Milk: Haiku Destinies.*

JULI JANA is a poet and academic living in London. She is also a visual poet and has an interest in history. Her work has appeared in several UK mags.

PAULA KONEAZNY lives in California. She has a chapbook, *Installation*, forthcoming from Tarpaulin Sky. She is an assistant editor of *VOLT*.

KAREN LEPRI, who lives on Cape Cod, holds an MFA in Literary Arts from Brown University. Her poems, translations, & reviews have appeared or are forthcoming in *Beloit Poetry Journal, Boston Review, Mandorla, Vanitas,* & *Word For/Word*, among others, & online at *Verse Daily*.

ROB A. MACKENZIE lives in Edinburgh. Salt published his first collection, *The Opposite of Cabbage*, in 2009. He is Reviews Editor for *Magma*.

IAN MCEWEN has had poems published in many magazines and in 2010 his pamphlet, *The Stammering Man*, was a winner in the Templar Competition. He lives in Bedford and is Treasurer of *Magma*.

JAMES MCLAUGHLIN lives in Dumbarton and has two chapbooks, *AEIDO* and *Text 1* from Knives, Forks & Spoons Press, Manchester.

JAMES MIDGLEY used to edit *Mimesis*, and won a Gregory Award in 2008. His work has appeared in *Horizon Review, Kenyon Review, Magma, New Welsh Review, Poetry Review, The Rialto* and *Stride*.

CAMILLA NELSON is studying for a PhD, *Reading and Writing with a Tree: Performing Nature Writing as Enquiry*, at University College Falmouth.

JENNIE OSBORNE's first full collection, *How to Be Naked*, was published in 2010 by Oversteps Press. She lives in Totnes, Devon.

JAN OWEN lives in South Australia. Her sixth book of verse *Poems 1980–2008* was published by John Leonard Press. She has a small virtual presence in the UK through her inclusion on the Poetry Archive website.

LINDA RUSSO is the author of *Mirth* (Chax Press) and several chapbooks, including *o going out* (Potes & Poets). Her poems have recently appeared in *New American Writing, Tinfish, ecopoetics, Interim*.

SAM SAMPSON's first collection, *everything talks*, was published in 2008 by Shearsman in the UK and Auckland University Press in New Zealand.

ALEXANDRA SASHE is based in Vienna, but was born in Moscow. A bilingual English/French collection of her poems, *Ver Sacrum*, is forthcoming.

NATHAN SHEPHERDSON lives in Queensland and is the author of several collections in Australia, including *Sweeping the Light* and *Apples with Human Skin* (both University of Queensland Press).

STEVEN TOUSSAINT is an American poet currently based in New Zealand. He has recently been published in *Cannibal, Jacket2 and Conjunctions*.

ROBERT VAS DIAS' *Still • Life* was published by Shearsman in 2010.

STEVEN WALING has published widely both as poet and as critic. *Travelator* was published by Salt (2007); *Captured Yes* by Knives, Forks & Spoons.

CHARLES WILKINSON has published *The Snowman and Other Poems* (Iron Press, 1987). Recent work has appeared in *Poetry Wales, Warwick Review, Tears in the Fence* and *Poetry Salzburg Review*, among others.

NICHOLAS YB WONG is the author of *Cities of Sameness* (Desperanto, 2012). He reads poetry for *Drunken Boat* and teaches in the Hong Kong Institute of Education.

www.ingramcontent.com/pod-product-compliance
Lightning Source LLC
Chambersburg PA
CBHW030958090426
42737CB00007B/583